They're the latest craze hitting the streets and playgrounds! If you miss them you're going to miss out,

so let's Go Go!

By the same author in Puffin Books

Fighting Fantasy

SPELLBREAKER

KNIGHTS OF DOOM

CURSE OF THE MUMMY

With Marc Gascoigne

SONIC THE HEDGEHOG: THEME PARK PANIC

SONIC THE HEDGEHOG: STORMIN' SONIC

Go Go's are Go Go!

The unofficial handbook

Jonathan Green

PUFFIN BOOKS

For Alex, Arif, Ashley, Ben, Chris, Cyrus, Jamie, Raman, Ravi,
Rikesh, Robin, Scott, Sonny and Thomas

With special thanks to Sarah Hughes and Richard Scrivener

PUFFIN BOOKS

Published by the Penguin Group
Penguin Books Ltd, 27 Wrights Lane, London W8 5TZ, England
Penguin Books USA Inc., 375 Hudson Street, New York, New York 10014, USA
Penguin Books Australia Ltd, Ringwood, Victoria, Australia
Penguin Books Canada Ltd, 10 Alcorn Avenue, Toronto, Ontario, Canada M4V 3B2
Penguin Books (NZ) Ltd, 182–190 Wairau Road, Auckland 10, New Zealand

Penguin Books Ltd, Registered Offices: Harmondsworth, Middlesex, England

First published 1997
1 3 5 7 9 10 8 6 4 2

Made and printed in England by Clays Ltd, St Ives plc

British Library Cataloguing in Publication Data
A CIP catalogue record for this book is available from the British Library

ISBN 0-140-38675-0

CONTENTS

WELCOME TO THE WONDERFUL WORLD OF GO GOs!

As if you didn't know already, Go Gos are the latest craze to hit the streets!

Yes, it's a full-scale invasion, with little plastic figures taking over playgrounds, classrooms and homes all over the country.

But what are Go Gos?

They are a gang of cool characters that you can play with or collect, or both! Each one has its own name, unique appearance and comical expression.

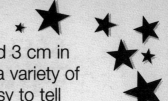

They are between 2.5 and 3 cm in height and they come in a variety of brilliant colours, so it's easy to tell them apart. They look great and they're fun to play with. In fact they are the latest, hippest form of a game that has been around for centuries. But more about the history later.

So what's the game?

You probably know already, but, just in case, each player throws three Go Gos or bones up into the air. You score points depending on which way your Go Gos land: face up, face down, on their sides or standing up. Whoever scores the most points wins the game.

It really couldn't be simpler.

THEM BONES, THEM BONES

You're probably thinking, they don't look much like bones to me. If my skeleton was made up of tiny bits of plastic I wouldn't be able to get up in the morning.

Now they might not *look* much like bones, even crazy ones, to you or me, but their name gives us a clue as to their secret past life. Yes, it's time to put on your FBI suit, talk in an American accent and open – the **Go Go Files!** The truth is out there.

The Secret Life of Bones

Let me take you on a journey through the secret history of Go Gos. Through the decades they have had many different disguises and names.

Knucklebones

Knucklebones was a very popular

game at around the time when your grandparents were your age. Knucklebones wasn't the only name for it though, it was also called Fivestones, Chuckstones, Jacks and Snobs. To play this game, you first have to get into a crouching position – very dignified, not! The crouching players then throw small objects into the air – does this sound familiar yet? – and try to catch them again in various peculiar ways. With each turn the ways the objects have to be caught get more difficult.

But it wasn't your grandparents who first played knucklebones. It wasn't even *their* grandparents, not even their great-great-grand . . .

Yes, all right, we get the idea. So who did first play the game?

Well, turn the page and I'll tell you.

Go, Greeks, Go!

Thousands of years ago the Greeks used the bones of dead animals to help them work out what fate had in store for them. They did this by throwing the bones into the air and seeing what patterns they made on the ground when they landed. Soon small bones painted with different numbers of spots on each side were being used in games from as far as Ancient Egypt to Ancient Rome.

Gradually other things, such as clay, wood and ivory, were used instead of bones. These small painted 'bones' went on to become the dice that we know today.

The first people to use six-sided dice, like the ones that you find in all sorts of games today, were the Arabs.

Yes, we can go!

So there you have it, the brilliant game you know today and the characters you play with are actually the hip nineties version of knucklebones. It's a game that has been around for centuries!

And now, with the help of this book, your favourite bones and a few pals, hours of fun lie ahead. Go on. Read on.

WHAT'S SO GREAT ABOUT GO GOs?

Maybe you've got a PlayStation, a PC, or you just enjoy watching TV. So why bother with a load of old bones?

You're kidding, right? They are the coolest thing since caps (and caps are still pretty cool). Everybody's gone bone-mad! Look around your school playground and see for yourself. Even the teachers are playing with them. Well, what do you think they do with the bones once they've confiscated them from you?

So why are they so popular? For starters, there are the crazy characters, funny expressions, wild colours and zany stickers. Also, you can play many different games with these cool bones,

and they look nice sitting on your window sill.

These guys are kind of cute. You don't *have* to throw them at each other. After all, that way you end up scratching their faces and they don't look as good. It could be just as rewarding to try to collect them all instead. You could always play against other people to win more bones for your collection, simply buy some new ones from the shops, or just swap with your friends. Whatever's the most fun.

GETTING STARTED

Where do you get them from?

You mean you don't know already?

Well, in case you've only just got back from a holiday on Venus, GoGo's® Crazy Bones® can be bought in newsagents and good toy shops all over the country. There's probably a store just around the corner or in your local high street that can't wait to supply you with all the GoGo's you could possibly want.

What do you get?

Once you've ripped open your packet you will find that it contains some official GoGo's. You will also find some cool stickers of GoGo's characters.

There are two series that you can buy:

Series One and Series Two. In each packet of both Series One and Series Two there is either one giant sticker or a card. The giant stickers have wacky pictures of crazy kids playing a game. The cards have large pictures of your favourite characters on them, or a checklist. These are handy for ticking off each one that you have in your collection and for seeing which ones you still need to get.

The main difference between the two series is the number of GoGo's and stickers that you get in each packet. In Series One packets you will find four GoGo's and four stickers, and in Series Two you will find two GoGo's and two stickers. Series One packets cost twice as much as Series Two, but you do get twice as many GoGo's!

They don't cost much

A packet of GoGo's® Crazy Bones® won't break the bank. In fact you'll probably still have change left after buying some with your pocket money. If you're not bothered about collecting the entire set and you just want to play for fun against your friends, you don't need anything else. You only need to buy one packet to get started. So get playing!

It doesn't take long to learn how to play

Like all the classic games, this one takes only seconds to learn but it can take weeks of practising before you are good enough to become a champion!

It's quick

It takes no time at all to set up and play a game of bones. The most basic game, with each player taking a turn, lasts about a minute, so there's plenty of time to have another go. You could

practise a few of the trickier shots, have a couple of warm-up games and then play an entire tournament in your lunch hour!

You can play anywhere

Well, almost anywhere. There's no booking of courts or checking that you've got the opening times right. Also you don't need to carry around a lot of special equipment before you can go out and play the game – just a few bones in your pocket will do. All you need is a suitable flat surface and a friend who's as crazy about bones as you are and you're away!

WHERE TO PLAY

Well, there's Wembley Stadium, the Royal Albert Hall and the National Exhibition Centre – they seem to be the really popular venues these days. But seriously, where you play your bone games can make a big difference to the outcome of a match.

What you really need in order to play a great game of bones is a solid, level surface. Your front doorstep, a pavement or a quiet corner of the playground, especially reserved for playing the latest cool crazes, is probably best. It ought to be smooth and flat. Just make sure you pick up the old crisp packets and apple cores that are obstructing the playing area and put them in the bin.

Playing at home

At home you need a smooth floor. Vinyl and wooden floors are both good. Carpet does not make a suitable playing surface as your bones will bounce about all over the place and shudder to a sudden stop. This may mean that your bedroom is not the best place to play, although up there you can keep out of everybody else's way and battle with your bones to your heart's content. However, don't play on the kitchen linoleum when dinner's being cooked and definitely not up against the newly painted skirting board! Outside, grass and the flower bed do not make good playing areas either, especially if it's wet!

Wherever you want to play, ultimately the best surface to play on is a game board. These are flat and smooth – the smoother the surface, the further your bones will slide. Game boards can be put down almost anywhere and they will protect whatever's underneath from damage.

Other places not to play

● On your parents carefully polished dining table. Nothing scratches that nice, smooth surface like a game of bones!

● In the car, especially if it's moving!

● Anywhere you can lose your precious, carefully collected bones!

Playing at school

School is the perfect place to play with your bones. All your friends who also happen to collect bones are there, there's plenty of time to play at break and there are perfect playing areas all over the place.

However, if you are going to play at school there are a few things worth thinking about first.

● If bones are not allowed in your school at all, or only under certain circumstances (like at lunch time), stick to the rule.

● Play fairly. If there are any arguments involving bones, you may find that your teachers ban them altogether. To be safe, only Play for Fun and not for Keeps.

● Don't take *all* your bones to school. Settle for a selection and preferably not all your favourite ones. That way, if you do Play for Keeps, you won't be tempted to risk letting someone win all your bones. Also if, horror of horrors, you *lose* them you won't have lost the entire set that it has taken you the last two months to collect.

Wherever you *do* play, whether at home or at school, make sure that you're not in anybody's way, and, most importantly, that where you're playing is safe.

BEFORE YOU PLAY

Now you know what bones are and where the game of Go Gos came from, it's time to get down to the nitty-gritty and start playing! But first, there're a few things that you need to know.

What do you need?

This bit couldn't be simpler. You need some bones, a friend or two and somewhere suitable to play (see page 18 for more details). What do you mean, your friends don't know how to play? Use this book to explain everything to them. Then you'll all be experts in no time!

How many can play?

Well, you need more than one player but less than ninety-nine – say about . . . two. Seriously though, depending on the rules that you're using, you can play

with two or more friends – up to about four is best. For individual rounds, especially for the basic games, it will probably be only two of you playing one-on-one. There will be times when more than two can play at once, but we'll get to that later.

How many bones do you need?

For most games you'll need only one bone at a time. However, you may want a few extra ready, to give you a choice of shooters and targets. Also, if you're going to play for keeps you'll need some bones in reserve that you wouldn't mind giving up to your opponent should you lose any games.

SHOOTERS AND TARGETS

This would be a good place to explain some of the 'technical' terms used in bones games.

The **Shooter** is a bone that is flicked or thrown to knock over other bones. It can also be called the **Hitter** or **Thrower.**

The **Target** is a bone that is being shot at. As you may have noticed, bones come in a variety of shapes, from round, fat ones to thin, slim ones. The shape and size of a bone can make all the difference to the outcome of a game.

Shooters

On the whole, the fatter and chunkier the shooter is, the more effective it will be. The extra weight and width make it more likely to hit the target and knock it over. It is also easier to control. There are some tall, wide bones that look as though they would make good shooters, but they don't always live up to expectations. They move quite slowly and when they hit another bone they tend to fall over flat on their backs. This makes the target less likely to fall over. For shooters the general rule is the shorter, squatter and rounder the better. It can sometimes be worth swapping several thinner or lighter bones for a chunkier one, as in the long run it will win back even more than you originally paid for it!

Targets

For a target you want to use a bone that presents the least surface area to be hit. The narrower it is, the harder it will be to hit. On the other hand, if you don't have any suitably thin bones, or they're your favourites, use one that you don't particularly like and don't mind losing. To add some excitement to your game, why not let your opponent choose which of your bones you use as the shooter and you can choose which of theirs will be the target.

FOR FUN OR FOR KEEPS?

Before you start playing there are a few things you need to agree with your friends.

Never mind all the alternative games and the various rules, there are really only two different ways you can play – for Fun or for Keeps!

Playing for Fun

Quite simply, if you're Playing for Fun, at the end of a game no one keeps any bones that weren't theirs to begin with. Any bones that you win gain you points that are added to your total score. The bones are then returned to their owner. It is a good idea to note down whose bones are whose before you start. Rather than the winner being the person who has won the most plastic figures, the player with the highest total score is declared the champion.

Playing for Keeps

If you Play for Keeps you get to keep the bones you win, but you have to be prepared to lose any that are won by an opponent. Playing for Keeps adds to the excitement of a game, but it does mean that you could lose *all* your carefully gathered bones. This isn't really very helpful if you are trying to build up your collection. Never Play for Keeps with your favourite bones! If you do Play for Keeps a good rule to use is that the first go is always just for fun and acts as a warm-up before you start playing seriously.

REMEMBER!

Make sure you decide whether you are going to Play for Fun or for Keeps before you start your game. That way there won't be any arguments and you won't suddenly find yourself with no bones at all! If someone won't Play for Fun when you ask them to, don't play with them at all!

WHO GOES FIRST?

Before you can start you need to work out who goes first. In some games, being the first to flick can mean the difference between winning and losing. To help you decide who that lucky someone is going to be, why not try out some of these methods?

Face Up, Face Down

This is an excellent way of deciding who goes first, as it uses the bones themselves. If you look closely at one of your crazy characters you will see that one side has a silly expression and the other doesn't. The side with the silly expression on it is the bone's 'face'. One player throws a bone up into the air. The other calls 'Face up' or 'Face down' before it lands. If the bone lands the way that the second player called, then they go first. If they got it wrong, the thrower goes first. If the bone lands on its side or stands upright, try again.

Best of Three

Follow the instructions as above, but this time follow your first throw with two more. The player who makes the most correct guesses goes first. Three throws are plenty – we do not recommend you try Best of Ninety-nine!

Chase the Bone

This is a good method if more than two people are playing. Each player puts one bone into a bag. You need to make sure that all the bones are different from each other, so that you can easily tell them apart. Then choose one bone to be the one to decide who starts the game. Without looking, the players take turns to pull one bone each out of the bag. Whoever picks the chosen bone starts the game.

Everyone has their own favourite way of deciding who goes first. Use the one that you and your pals are happiest with, but make sure that it's fair.

LET'S PLAY!

You've got your bones ready and a friend with bones too, so let's play

The Basic Game

The basic game couldn't be easier to learn, especially if you follow this simple guide.

1 The first player throws three of his bones up into the air and lets them land again.

2 Depending on how the bones land the player scores a different number of points. The points are worked out like this. If the bone lands face down it is said to be 'dead' and so scores no points. If it lands face up you score one point. If the bone lands lying on its side you score two points, as this is less likely to happen. Should the bone land standing up, which is very unlikely, this is called an 'ace' and scores you a massive five points!

3   The player adds up the total number of points scored by all three of the bones put together.

4   Each of the other players then has their turn, throwing three of their bones into the air and adding up the points they score when they land.

5   The winner is the player with the highest score. If there is a tie, with two or more of the players having the highest score, those players must play again until one of them wins. What could be simpler?

If you are Playing for Keeps, the winner is allowed to take one bone from each of the losers. This rule applies to all bone games, unless we tell you otherwise.

Once you've played the basic game a few times you might want to try out some of these variations to increase the risk and the excitement.

Toss them Bones

This version is quite simply the basic game with several turns, rather than just one. At the start of the game, the players agree how many turns the game will last. Each of the players then takes turns to throw their bones as before, but when the last player has thrown, the first starts again. The total score from all the turns decides the winner.

Up the Odds

This is the same as the basic game except for one major difference. Once a player has thrown their bones, if they score a total of two points or more in that turn they do not have to end their go. If the player wants to, they may throw their bones again. Any points that are scored are then added to a running total for that turn. However, if during the player's go their bones score less than two points in total on one turn, their total score is wiped out and play automatically passes to the next player. On their next go they must start from zero again! If they decide not to risk losing all the points scored so far, they can stop at any time, and play then passes to the next player.

Chuck-in

For this variation, each of the players puts in the same number of bones. They then take turns to throw them all up into the air at once. Each player works out what their own bones, not anyone else's, have scored each time they are thrown. Those scores are then added together and, you've guessed it, the highest score wins.

BONE BOWLING

You've tried all the versions of the basic game and you're ready for something else? OK, let's get bowling!

Bowling Bones

This is another popular and fun game to play with your bones. Also, rather than being purely a game of chance, bone bowling requires a certain amount of skill. You'll need lots of practice. This is how you play.

1 Each player puts down the same number of bones to use as targets. Three or four is a good number.
2 Stand the bones upright on the playing surface, quite close to a wall.
3 The players take turns to throw one bone directly at all the others in an attempt to knock over as many as possible. The targets are placed upright again between each player's go.

4   Every bone belonging to someone else that is knocked over by a player scores one point.

5   Any of the player's own bones that are knocked over do not count towards their score and are simply replaced in their starting positions.

6   The player who has scored the most points after three throws each is declared the winner.

HANDY HINT

When you are bone bowling, it is easier to tell one player's bones from another's if each player uses bones of one colour only or one character only. Obviously you won't be able to do this unless your collection is big enough.

OK, so you've got your eye in and you want to liven up your bowling games. Well, read on.

Bowled Over

You play this bowling game exactly as just described, except each bone that is knocked over scores points depending on how it lands, as in the basic game (see page 30).

Ten-bone Bowling

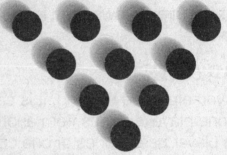

Shoot at this end

Ten bones are set out in a triangle as shown above (it doesn't matter who they belong to). The players take turns to bowl but each gets two shots in their turn. Each bone that's knocked over scores one point. Before the next player's turn, the bones are stood up again in their original positions. After

everyone has had ten turns the one
with the highest score wins.

Strike Out!

WARNING! This one is for experts! Set
up the bones in the same way as you
would for Ten-bone Bowling, but before
you start bowling nominate three bones
that must *not* be knocked over! The
players then bowl as normal, but for
each of the no-go bones that is
knocked over one point is deducted
from that player's score.

Why not try . . .

● Spinning the bone by twisting it
between your fingers and thumb as you
throw it. This makes the bone rebound
all over the place, hopefully knocking
over more of the targets!

● Throwing two bones at once. It's not
as easy as it sounds.

● Rolling the bone along the ground at
the others. You'll need to give it quite a
hard push.

BATTLING BONES

One of the most popular games to play is the one-on-one battle! It tests your skill as a bones player as well as your hand and eye coordination. Are you ready to take up the challenge?

One-on-one

This is one of the most exciting bones games that you can play. This is what you do.

1 Two players each stand one bone at opposite ends of the playing area, about one metre apart.

2 Player One flicks, knocks or slides their bone (the shooter) at their opponent's.

3 If the shooter hits the target bone and knocks it over, Player One wins the point. (If you are Playing for Keeps, they get to keep the knocked-over bone.)

4 It is now Player Two's turn, whether Player One knocked over the target or not. Player One stands their bone at

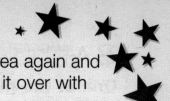

their end of the playing area again and Player Two tries to knock it over with their shooter.

Take as many turns as you like until you have run out of time or run out of bones to play with!

GoGo's® Battle

This is a larger version of the One-on-one game as suggested by the makers of GoGo's, and is very exciting as lots of bones can be lost or won.

1   Player One sets up a line of six bones, each one several centimetres apart, at their end of the playing area.
2   Player Two then sets up their own line about two metres away from that of Player One.
3   Player One flicks or hits one of their bones at the other player's line, trying to knock Player Two's bones down.
4   Player Two then does the same to Player One's bones.

5 Play continues for as long as you want, but each of the players must have the same number of turns.
6 The players keep any bones that they knock over. If they're not Playing for Keeps they score one point for each bone knocked over instead.

As well as the different battles that you can have with your bones, here are some extra rules that you might want to use to add a twist to your games.

Knock-out!

If the shooter leaves the playing area when it has knocked over the target both pieces go to the target player!

Penalty

This rule applies if the shooter hits the target a glancing blow but doesn't knock it over. When the target player takes their turn they take the shot from halfway down the playing area. As they are that much closer to the new target

The Nudge

This can be more accurate than the flick. Put your first two or three fingers together with your thumb behind them and give the shooter a sharp shove with your fingernails. On the down side it can be hard getting enough power into the nudge shot.

The Hit

This is known as one of the most common methods of shooting. To do it, cup your hand slightly and hit the bone with either the inside of the fingers or your palm. It can be a very powerful shot but it's also hard to control where the shooter goes.

The Knock

This is achieved by hitting the shooter with the side of your hand while sliding the hand, held palm down, over the ground towards the bone. The knock is quite a powerful shot if done with enough force.

The Shove

It's always best to do this where there is an edge to the playing surface, for example if you are playing on a table top. Put the shooter next to the table rim, so that the back of it just hangs over the edge slightly, then give it a hard push with the palm of your hand. The shove is good for covering distance but it can be a little tricky to set up.

The Slide

Holding the shooter between your first finger and thumb, slide it along the ground and then let go, giving it an extra little push. WARNING! Some players see this move as cheating. Check that your opponent doesn't mind you using the slide before you start your game!

REMEMBER!

The best way of shooting won't be the same for everybody. Try out some of these techniques and then use the one

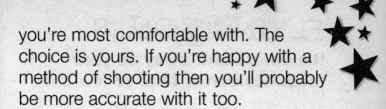

you're most comfortable with. The choice is yours. If you're happy with a method of shooting then you'll probably be more accurate with it too.

Whoops!

If you hit the shooter and it flies off away from you and your target, you have sliced it! Alternatively, if when you hit the shooter it flies towards you, again missing the bone or bones you were aiming for, you've hooked it! If you can help it, you don't want to do either, as you're likely to lose the game!

How hard?

Knowing how hard to hit your shooter is something that only comes with practice and experience. It depends on a lot of factors such as the weight of the bone you are using as the shooter, its shape and the surface you're playing on. Once you've played lots of games, it will become easier for you to judge the best way to hit it.

FLYING BONES

It's up, up and away as your favourite bones take to the air!

Flying Bones is another game that is very similar to the original game of knucklebones but which uses the colourful characters that we all know and love. Here's what you do.

1 The first player must throw one bone into the air, pick up another one from the ground and catch the first bone in the same hand before it lands.
2 The next player then does the same.
3 Once all the players have had a go it is the first player's turn again. This time the number of bones he has to pick up from the ground increases by one.
4 The next player then tries to pick up the same number of bones as the first player before catching his first piece!

5   If a player fails to pick up the right number of bones or doesn't catch the one they threw on its way down then they are out.

6   Play continues with the number of bones to be picked up increasing by one each round.

7   The last person left in is the winner. If the last two players fail the same throw they must try the same throw again until one of them is the winner.

This is a good game for two people to play, although Flying Bones can be played with any number of players. However, if you have more than four you start having to wait a while for your turn to come round again. That isn't very exciting, and the whole point of playing is to have some fun, otherwise you might as well watch paint dry or the grass grow!

TARGET GAMES

This is where things get a little confusing. When we talk about target games we don't mean 'target' in the same way we do when talking about battling bones games. In this case think of the kind of target that you would aim at in archery or darts – it's a circular or rectangular grid separated into areas that have different points values. The bigger the area, the easier it is to hit, so it is worth fewer points. The smaller, more difficult areas to hit are worth more.

Fabulous glossy game boards that will last for ages are available from the makers of GoGo's® Crazy Bones® and others can be found in some puzzle magazines. Of course, there's nothing to stop you making your own. You can use paper or card and brightly coloured

felt tips or, if you want, just settle for a
chalk grid drawn on the pavement.
There are not many rules to learn
before you can play a target game. In
general they are as follows.

1   The target is placed flat on the
ground and the players agree between
them how far from it they should stand
before they throw.
2   The players each take turns to
throw one of their bones at the target.
They score the number of points that
the area they land on is worth.
3   If a bone lands between sections,
the lowest score is taken. If the bone
lands outside the target area the player
scores nothing.
4   The player with the most points
after a certain number of throws
(normally three) is the winner.

If you are Playing for Keeps, the winner
takes one bone from each of the
losers.

BONEBALL

Do you like sending small metal balls hurtling around pinball tables? If so, then this game is for you! Actually you'll love this game whether you like pinball or not.

To play Boneball you will need between five and ten bones to use as targets (it doesn't matter whose they are), and one shooter. You will also find some thick books, like telephone directories, small boxes or pieces of wood useful.

The first thing you need to do is set up your Boneball table. Lay your books or pieces of wood down so that they make three sides of a square. An area 30 cm by 30 cm is about right (by the way, 30 cm is the length of a telephone directory). This is your playing area. To make the game more interesting, you then need to place an obstacle about the size of a half a house brick in the

centre of the area. Next place your bones at regular intervals around the square and you are ready to play.

Books or wood   **Obstacle**

Bones

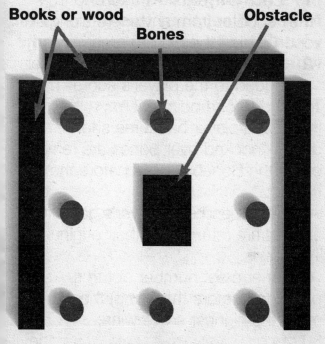

Shoot from here

So you've got your Boneball table set up, you've selected your shooter and your index finger's itching to flick. You're ready to play.

How to play

It really couldn't be easier.

1 Each player takes a turn to flick their shooter from anywhere along the open end of the playing area.

2 Any bones that are knocked over are added to the player's score. They are worth one point each.

3 Each player has three shots in a turn. Knocked over bones are removed from the Boneball table before the next shot.

4 At the end of a player's go all the bones are returned to their original positions.

5 After a set number of turns (decided before the game) the player with the highest score wins.

Boneball Bonkers!

To vary your Boneball games why not try some of these variations.

● Change the layout of the Boneball table, adding more obstacles and

changing the position of the targets.

● Add up the numbers stamped on the back of the bones that are knocked over to give the players' scores.

● Try flicking two shooters up the table at the same time!

● Change the number of target bones on the table at one time.

● Replace the bones that are knocked over in one go in their original places before the player's next shot to get some really high scores.

● Increase the size of the Boneball table. Remember you'll need a larger boundary, more obstacles, more bones and you'll have to hit the shooters harder!

STICK 'EM UP!

Of course, when you buy a packet of GoGo's® you don't just get some little plastic buddies for your money. There are also a couple of great stickers, but what can you do with them? Well, rather than plaster them all over your bedroom walls, play some games with them.

If you are going to play games with your stickers it's usually helpful if you peel them off their backing paper first and stick them on to some thin card. This will make them last longer and, as you may have noticed, the backs are printed with a number that could lead to cheating.

Mix and Match

A game suggested by the makers of GoGo's is the old chestnut of matching the cards. You will need pairs of cards with the same stickers on them. You then shuffle the cards and lay them out on a table, face down, in a rectangular pattern. The players take turns to turn over two of the cards at a time. If the stickers on the cards are the same, the player keeps the pair and has another go. If the cards are not the same they are turned over again and it is the next player's turn. When all the pairs have been collected, the player with the most cards wins.

Snap!

It may be old, but it's still a fun game, especially if you play it with pictures of your favourite GoGo's® characters. For those of you who don't know how to play, everyone is dealt the same number of cards and players then take turns to lay down one card at a time. If a card matches the one put down last, the first person to shout 'Snap!' wins the whole pile. The player who manages to end up with all the cards is the winner.

TOURNAMENTS

Can't decide who's the greatest bones player? Are you arguing about who's the master of the flick? Then why not play your own tournament?

Tournaments are a great way to decide once and for all who's the Bones Champion among your friends. They're also great fun and a great excuse to play even more games! All you need is a group of friends who want to challenge each other to bone games and one person who is willing to act as the umpire. The umpire keeps the score and makes sure that everyone else plays fairly. Any of the games suggested for playing with bones can be used in a tournament, just make sure that everyone is playing the same one!

The other thing to remember is that

games should only be played between two people at a time. At the start of the tournament everyone is paired up with another player, so you will need an even number of people to take part. The players in each pair then play each other, and the winner goes on to meet another winner from the same round. This continues through to quarter-finals, semi-finals and the grand final itself. Whoever wins this is declared the Bones Champion!

It is best if you only Play for Fun in a tournament. The umpire keeps the scores for the individual games and he determines who wins. This way, the grand champion doesn't end up with everyone else's bones!

BONES IN OTHER GAMES

There are board games available specifically for bones. The boards are great fun, with cool graphics and bright colours, while the games themselves have all sorts of extra rules and hazards to keep you on your toes. But you aren't restricted to using your bones just in bone games. Oh no!

Imagine the scene. It's a wet Sunday afternoon, Grandma's dozing in the chair by the fire, there's absolutely nothing on TV and you're bored out of your mind. Then someone suggests a game of . . . Ludo! How dull. This is the video age, such old-fashioned board games just don't seem as much fun as they once were. Or do they?

Why not liven up your old board games by using your brightly coloured bones as the playing pieces? They're more exciting than those half-chewed bits of plastic that look like tiddlywinks, and they make a change from a silver top hat or a Scottie dog.

What about a game of Draughts (or Chequers as it's also known), but with smiling plastic figures jumping over each other rather than discs of black and white wood (there are always at least three missing from every set anyway). For doubles put two bones down together in one square. Just make sure you know whose pieces are whose!

If you're feeling really brave you could try a game of Bone Chess: 'Now, that spray can is a knight and can move two squares forward and one to the side. What's the typewriter again? Is it a bishop or a pawn?'

Go on then, your old copy of Snakes and Ladders is just waiting to be revitalized with your latest zany figures!

LOOKING AFTER YOUR BONES

Whether you're using your bones to play tournaments or you just want to collect them, it is still important that you look after them.

First of all, if you're a serious bones fan, it's useful if you have something to keep them in. When you have so many lumps of plastic to carry around with you, suddenly your pocket doesn't seem to be quite large enough. Old plastic bags won't really do either, as these can be easily torn.

To keep your bones safe you need something that can be closed securely, such as a unused pencil case or an empty ice-cream tub. You can then decorate the container with all those marvellous stickers you've collected along with your bones. If you're feeling really creative you could even make yourself a simple cloth bag with a drawstring top. Then, when you turn up in the playground and issue a challenge, you'll really look like you mean business!

Swapping bones

What do you do with all those extra bones you end up with that look the same, feel the same and are in fact exactly the same as half the others you've got? Spares can be used as targets when you are playing games for keeps. Swapping your spares with your friends can be a good way of building up your collection and getting hold of that one character that you've always wanted. Sometimes people will swap several bones for just one that they really want. If you do this, make sure that the bone you're getting is really worth the cost! Maybe it's an excellent shooter or it's the last one you need to complete your magnificent collection.

You've read *the* book, you're bursting with ideas for new games you want to try out, so pick up your trusty bones, find some friends and start playing!

It's time to get Go Going!

READ MORE IN PUFFIN

For children of all ages, Puffin represents quality and variety – the very best in publishing today around the world.

For complete information about books available from Puffin – and Penguin – and how to order them, contact us at the appropriate address below. Please note that for copyright reasons the selection of books varies from country to country.

On the worldwide web: www.penguin.co.uk

In the United Kingdom: Please write to *Dept. EP, Penguin Books Ltd, Bath Road, Harmondsworth, West Drayton, Middlesex UB7 0DA*

In the United States: Please write to *Consumer Sales, Penguin USA, P.O. Box 999, Dept. 17109, Bergenfield, New Jersey 07621-0120*. VISA and MasterCard holders call 1-800-253-6476 to order Penguin titles

In Canada: Please write to *Penguin Books Canada Ltd, 10 Alcorn Avenue, Suite 300, Toronto, Ontario M4V 3B2*

In Australia: Please write to *Penguin Books Australia Ltd, P.O. Box 257, Ringwood, Victoria 3134*

In New Zealand: Please write to *Penguin Books (NZ) Ltd, Private Bag 102902, North Shore Mail Centre, Auckland 10*

In India: Please write to *Penguin Books India Pvt Ltd, 706 Eros Apartments, 56 Nehru Place, New Delhi 110 019*

In the Netherlands: Please write to *Penguin Books Netherlands bv, Postbus 3507, NL-1001 AH Amsterdam*

In Germany: Please write to *Penguin Books Deutschland GmbH, Metzlerstrasse 26, 60594 Frankfurt am Main*

In Spain: Please write to *Penguin Books S. A., Bravo Murillo 19, 1° B, 28015 Madrid*

In Italy: Please write to *Penguin Italia s.r.l., Via Felice Casati 20, I–20124 Milano*

In France: Please write to *Penguin France S. A., 17 rue Lejeune, F–31000 Toulouse*

In Japan: Please write to *Penguin Books Japan, Ishikiribashi Building, 2–5–4, Suido, Bunkyo-ku, Tokyo 112*

In South Africa: Please write to *Longman Penguin Southern Africa (Pty) Ltd, Private Bag X08, Bertsham 2013*